The Way We Looked

The Way We Looked

THE MEANING

AND MAGIC

OF FAMILY PHOTOGRAPHS

Catherine Noren

LODESTAR BOOKS
E. P. Dutton   New York

The author and publisher have made every effort to trace
ownership of all photographs contained herein. It is their
belief that the necessary permissions from the owners have been
obtained. In the event of any questions arising as to the use of
any material, the author and publisher express regret for any
error unconsciously made and will be pleased to make the
necessary corrections in future editions of the book.

All photographs not otherwise credited
are from the collection of the author.

Copyright © 1983 by Catherine Noren

LIBRARY OF CONGRESS CATALOGING IN PUBLICATION DATA
Noren, Catherine.
The way we looked.
"Lodestar books."
Includes index.
Summary: Discusses the importance of family
photographs as a means of understanding the passage of
time, establishing ties with ancestors, and varying
ways of recording important events in family life.
Includes suggestions for collecting photographs and
putting together an album.
1. Photography of families—Juvenile literature.
[1. Photography of families.   2. Photography]   I. Title.
TR681.F28N67   1983   778.9'2   82-9682
ISBN 0-525-66738-5

Published in the United States by E. P. Dutton, Inc.,
2 Park Avenue, New York, N.Y. 10016
Published simultaneously in Canada by Clarke,
Irwin & Company Limited, Toronto and Vancouver
EDITOR: Virginia Buckley   DESIGNER: Trish Parcell

Printed in the U.S.A.   First Edition
10 9 8 7 6 5 4 3 2 1

Acknowledgements

Warmest thanks to my aunt, Annelise Wallach Rosenberg, family photographer and documentarian, for giving me access to her enormous archive; to Amy Kotkin and Steven Zeitlin of the Smithsonian Institution's Office of Folklife Programs for the use of photographs from the Smithsonian collection; and to Samuel Menashe, for the use of his lovely poem about his mother, which appears on page 26. His mother is the central figure in the photograph on the front of the jacket.

to my mother,
Lotte Wallach Hanf,
with my love
and deep appreciation of
her generosity and courage

LISEL HAAS

Contents

Chapter One

What Family Photographs Show Us

Family photographs possess a special magic. They are different from other kinds of photographs. Their appeal, their uniqueness, is partly due to a mystery, the mystery of existence. When I look at an old photograph of my great-grandmother or my great-aunt, I get a tremendous thrill just having positive proof that these people really did live once. When I was a child, I didn't believe that anybody had existed before my lifetime; even now, I tend to think of the people around me as having always been the way I know them in the present. When I haven't seen friends for a long time, I always think that they will look just the way they did when I last saw them—and I'm always surprised when they don't. Family photographs enable me to see how my relatives looked, dressed, sat, and felt about one another and themselves.

Before the invention of photography, we had only the imaginations of painters and the descriptive words of writers to tell us what the past was like. Imagination, even when it's combined with memory, is at best an inaccurate way of recording history. But with the invention of photography in 1839, we were able, for the first time in history, to make reasonably accurate images of people, places, and events as they actually were.

Today we take photography for granted. It is so much a part of our everyday lives that it is almost impossible to imagine what a miracle it must have been to the first photographers and their subjects.

Everybody has family photographs. If they are not carefully mounted in albums that live in a bookcase in the guest room, then they are probably lying around in the back of the drawer that also has rubber bands, erasers, pencils, old mailing labels, and flashlights with dead batteries. They are old Kodak prints from the forties, curly edged 3 by 5's taken with 1963 Instamatics, Polaroid snapshots from last Christmas. The older photographs—paper prints on cardboard mounts—are carefully framed and hung in a corner of the living room. Class photos of school children are carried by Mother in her handbag, by Dad in his wallet or inside jacket pocket.

These photos are priceless. Not that anyone would pay

The day you and your brothers got your New York Yankees uniforms. Each time you look at that old snapshot, you remember the pleasure of the event. COURTESY MARK SILK

you for that old picture of you and your brothers on the day you got your New York Yankees uniforms. But its enormous value is in its connection to your own memory of that day. What a wonderful time the three of you had! What good friends you were! No amount of money could buy those feelings.

· 3 ·

Family photographs are not only the storage places of our memories, they also tell us what we're probably going to look like forty years from now. They are our version of a time machine. Let me explain what I mean: Old family photographs give us proof of our roots. They give us clues as to who we were in the past. We see our own features— hands, eyes, ears, chins, cheeks, noses—and our own bodies —tall and thin, broad and square, short and fat—recycled through the generations until they reappear in us. They show us all the other members of our genetic clan.

Physical likeness is often handed down from one generation to the next. These women, two generations apart in the same family, are a great-aunt and her great-niece. They never met; in fact, the aunt died the year before her niece was born. But look at the resemblance.

LEFT: ADOLPH SCHINDELER, COLLECTION OF THE AUTHOR;
RIGHT: ANNELISE WALLACH ROSENBERG

In the photographs of our family members growing from babyhood to adulthood to old age, we can see proof that time exists, and we have a record of its passage. Kings, philosophers, scientists, artists, and most particularly old people have declared that of all the gifts they desired, time would be the greatest gift of all. Time, a commodity that cannot be defined in any tangible way, cannot be bought, cannot be seen, cannot be held in your hands. But without it, nothing—none of your other gifts—could be enjoyed. It's an experience. The invention of photography has given us, at last, a way of measuring it visually.

In the family photographs that we cherish so, we are able to "freeze" time, to "stop" it, and in this way to control it. This time-freezing machine lets me see my mother the way she looked as a baby, as a teenager, as a young bride. It lets me see her as she was when she was younger than I am now.

Family photographs—both snapshots and formal portraits—sometimes seem to make time shorter or to erase it. Because they make it possible to bring everyone into the present—to make dead relatives come alive—they actually help to turn time into a place! When I look at photographs of my great uncle as a sixteen-year-old boy, he isn't just from another time, he's from another place. I get the feeling that my long dead relatives are simply living somewhere else, and these photographs I gaze at so intently bring them here. One of the barriers that keeps me from them is eliminated. I move closer to all those people from my past.

Family photographs give us a chance to relive our happiest memories. They convince us that our lives are happy and have always been happy. It seems to be a tradition of human behavior to do nothing to preserve or remember the bad times. How many photographs do you have of family funerals? Photographs taken at a hospital sickbed? Photographs of your uncle on the terrible day he lost his job? Photographs of a relative at the front in Vietnam?

The passage of time, as we can see it in one person growing from babyhood to adulthood, is shown here. On the opposite page: top left, *Steven, two years old, is being protected and sheltered by his father;* top right, *five-year-old Steven is learning to exercise one of his talents;* below, *Steven,* second from left, *plays a fifties "greaser" in a camp show.* On this page: *Twenty-four-year-old Steven appears as an equal with his father.*

ANNELISE WALLACH ROSENBERG

We almost always choose to remember only the good times, and this we do through photographs of special occasions, celebrations, and the high moments of our lives. The fact that history repeats itself may be related to this tradition. If we could choose to remember, and remember well, some of the very worst of times, perhaps we wouldn't have so many of them. That's why, as we look through old photographs, the lives of our family members appear to have been continuously happy. In some way, family photographs help us to believe that life is good, abundant, and happy, and that all the people in our families are full of love and good feelings for each other and the world.

This photograph defies a tradition of family photography. It was taken in Germany in 1915 and sent to relatives in America who, because of World War I, could not attend the funeral.

COURTESY PAUL REIMERS

We see Dad bravely serving his country, but we are never shown how much he may have suffered during the war.

COURTESY ANN HAWKINS

The fact that we take them ourselves makes us love family photographs even more. When we push the shutter button, we become the instant historians of our families. We are the ones who determine how others will remember us. In the subjects we choose, the occasions and events, in how we compose our photographs, in what we include or decide to leave out, we determine how our families will be perceived by future generations. We play a very important role.

In the following chapters, I will talk about how you can learn about your family through the photographic images they have kept of themselves. I'll give you some suggestions about how to put together a visual family tree—a story of the evolution of your family and its passage through time —by composing and assembling a sequence of images, a narrative of your family's evolution and descent. I'll talk about what kinds of photographs to look for, what words and text you'll want to use with your photographs, where to look for what you want, how you'll know when you've found it, and how and where to get the supplementary verbal and historical information you'll need. Also, how to interview family members, how to ask them to lend you their photographs, which photographs to ask for, how to interpret what you get, how to look at family photographs with a new and different eye—an eye to gleaning all kinds of details that the official genealogy of your family would never tell you. And finally, how to learn about relationships among family members—who were the family favorites, who were the family scapegoats, who played what psychological role. I'll also give you suggestions about how to save, store, index, and take proper care of your own photos and borrowed material.

Family photographs are about everybody's favorite subject—riches. They are about all kinds of riches and wealth —financial wealth, psychological wealth, and emotional wealth. They are another way of saying love.

Chapter Two

How Photography
Came of Age

Before the invention of photography, people immortalized their mothers, fathers, husbands, wives, sons, daughters, and themselves in paintings. A portrait painter was commissioned, and the subject was carefully dressed, combed, arranged, set up and draped in an appropriate setting, together with pets, pieces of furniture, and other objects of significance. Each element was chosen to lend character and personality to the subject and to reveal his or her financial and social status. What the painter intended to capture in these portraits was the essence of the subject's personality. He tried to paint the subject in a typical mood, in favorite (usually elegant) clothing, and surrounded by meaningful objects. For these reasons and others that had to do with the painter and his style, such portraits were always unrealistic, never true to life.

A major difference between the painted family portrait and the one made for the camera is in price. Portrait paintings were a luxury available only to the well-to-do. On the other hand, within a short time after their invention, photographs could be produced cheaply enough to make them available to most families. Photography is a much more democratic medium than painting.

Family photographs had, as their emotional ancestors, the Renaissance family portrait, painted in oil and available only to the financially privileged. Wealth and dignity were the primary qualities these portraits were designed to transmit about their subjects, for dignity and prosperity were considered the ultimate in what was desirable in life. When the first family photographs were made, they automatically picked up on this tradition started centuries earlier.

One hundred years ago, people dressed themselves in all their best—and sometimes only—finery, went to a fashionable studio, and posed with all their most valuable assets (usually children) for the photographer, their friends, and for their descendants, born and unborn.

A typical family portrait of the late twentieth century observes an almost totally opposite tradition.

As photographic technology began to grow up, starting with the photographs of the 1920s, we could begin to see more and more of the daily activities our families used to enjoy—walking, horseback riding, traveling about the countryside, pumping water from a well.

In 1888, when Kodak introduced the first box camera— "You push the button; we do the rest"—it brought the camera out of the studio once and for all. It was these cameras that began the boom in amateur photography, a boom that is *still* growing. Anyone could shoot pictures. The camera began to travel with us wherever we went. It began, for the first time, to be used to document activities and outings.

Typical family portrait of the late nineteenth century

Typical family portrait of the late twentieth century

CATHERINE NOREN

Photography became an immensely popular hobby with the manufacture of cameras inexpensive enough for most middle-class people to afford and simple enough for most people to operate. The variety of subjects considered suitable for the camera's lens increased enormously.

Today, whatever we are doing, whenever we're doing it, is considered fair game for the camera. Thirty-five millimeter negatives, mass production of prints, blowups, cheap film, color film, the Instamatic camera, and especially the Polaroid and its equivalents have made everything—even the tiniest details of an ordinary day—instantly available for recording and preserving. With changing times and changing technology, our whole notion of what's appropriate for the camera has also changed, and it is difficult to say which changed first. Today we even photograph people sitting on the toilet—a situation that seventy-five years ago would have been not only unthinkable, but unspeakable.

The photograph below, taken around 1924, is an early example of action photography.
MORITZ WALLACH, COLLECTION OF THE AUTHOR

At right: *On outings to the countryside, the camera now went along.*

COURTESY BETTY LIDDLE

Lower right: *Our once much desired sense of dignity has been replaced in importance by a sense of humor.*

Above: *With the development of candid photography, we got very busy for the camera.*　COURTESY ALICE TAYLOR

Below: *What an incredible sight it once was to see someone we knew and loved in such an exotic locale! The date is 1922, the place is Egypt, and the woman is a young American bride on her honeymoon.*　COURTESY MARY SCHIEFFELIN

Pleasure and good times are the messages of today's snap-shots. Today, most of all, we photograph the pursuit of happiness. We want the world to know that we've been successful in this pursuit. And as our standards of happiness change, so do our photographs. Once we wanted to transmit the image of an upright family—closely knit, prosperous, and serious about life and purpose. In those days we

Family photographs display assets, showing where family members have been and what they own. Left: *The Leaning Tower of Pisa.* COURTESY MR. AND MRS. FRED WALLACE

Below: *This man has one daughter, two horses, one mule, and a hired hand.*
COURTESY RON SUTTON

were well dressed, well lit, well arranged, and willing to sit very still for the camera to record these qualities.

With the development of the candid camera in the 1930s, we stopped being so still and started to get very busy. Today, we are primarily interested in showing how much time we have and how we fill every minute of it.

Family photos are really advertisements for family life. This photograph, taken at the 1964 wedding of his granddaughter Carolyn Quackenbush, in Port Jervis, New York, shows the descendants of Dr. Henry Swartwout. COURTESY MARTHA SWARTWOUT

Christmas photographs are a celebration of good things and good feelings. They're about generosity and love.

We started walking, running, biking, dancing, and jumping into swimming pools. We wanted to show the world all the places we had been: Vacation photography grew immensely popular as the camera shrunk small enough to travel. We wanted the camera to show all the things we could do: climb a mountain, swim a lake, win a dance marathon. The perfect photograph of how prosperous we are is called *Christmas by the tree.*

So, in a way, things haven't changed. Family photographs still display assets. The assets may be as subtle as "Look where I've been!"—or as obvious as "Look what I've got!" They show our emotional assets—happiness, closeness, and love.

When photography was very young and its existence still a miracle of invention and a marvel of imagination, a major part of its magic was that it showed us sights, places, and events that we had never seen and never expected to see. Photography brought the whole world into our living rooms and *showed* us what before we had only been told about—the pyramids of ancient Egypt, the Great Wall of China, the Taj Mahal, Calcutta's teeming crowds, the great cathedrals of Europe. We could at last lay eyes on what was strange, alien, and other—all the things that were outside our personal experience.

As technology—the invention of television and motion pictures—has made the world in our living rooms an everyday occurrence, the standards of photography, as well as its uses, have changed. Today, when technology enables us to look at the surface of the moon, the rings of Saturn, and the floor of the ocean, we turn to still photographs to give us different sorts of information—to show us inner worlds, inner truths, inner likenesses and differences. Now that we know what the exterior, the surface of everything looks like, what we want to know next is, What do things feel like? How do other people experience their lives? How do they react? What is their emotional climate? What do they look like in the privacy of their bathrooms and kitchens—and in the privacy of their souls? With the disappearance of all other frontiers, the frontier of privacy is also disappearing. Inner worlds have been declared fair game for the camera. While travel and vacation photography are still as popular as they ever were, inner space is the newest territory that invites us to explore it.

Family photos still also show us the traditional subjects that we know and love. And in some ways, these subjects have become even more important than they ever were, because everything else is changing so much. Even our families are changing. As our families become less intimate and spend less time together, we have a great need for photographs that remind us so wonderfully of good times spent together. With single families now becoming multiple or extended families, with mothers and fathers and daughters and sons living in different households, we need lots of photographs to show what everybody looks like, and what they're doing, and how they're doing. It's lucky that we can mass-produce them so cheaply, because so many people need prints!

Chapter Three

Learning a Visual Vocabulary

When we read family photographs, the kinds of information the images yield is different from the kinds of information given us by words. Or, to put it more accurately, we get at visual information in a different way. The first rule of a photographic vocabulary is that everything in the frame counts. No matter how small or seemingly insignificant the detail, object, or element, it might be important and therefore must not be overlooked. In order to be able to see everything that is there, buy yourself a magnifying glass, such as a jewelers' loupe. With this, you can catch the tiny details that are so easy to overlook with the naked eye. It is often in such details that the real story or at least some vital clues lie. Two photographs will illustrate what I mean:

In one photograph, Susan is posing with her father, her sister, and some camp friends. In the other photo, she is posing with her mother, her sister, and some camp friends.

After having studied these two photographs, we can now say which of her parents Susan identifies with most. Susan's role model is her father. Look at the way Susan, *second from right,* is sitting in both photographs. Knees apart, legs wide, and elbows hanging, Susan imitates her father's posture even when she is next to her mother. Down to the expression on her face, Susan is clearly the tomboy. Her sister, *second from left,* with crossed ankles, is the "lady." In both photographs, Susan's sister imitates their feminine mother. When I asked Susan to confirm my observations, she did so without hesitating.

COURTESY SUSAN NORTON

Before you read further in this book, what do you know about these people just by looking at the photograph?

There are two things one notices immediately about this photograph of two women and a man. The first is that it was not taken in this country. Both the clothes and the faces are foreign. In fact, it was taken in Bessarabia, a part of Eastern Europe that now belongs to Russia.

The other thing that is immediately noticeable is that everybody is touching somebody else. Another photograph I saw of this family confirmed for me that this is one of the touchingest families I have ever come across. Whether it was typical of that part of the world or only of this particular family, I have yet to find out.

The same woman as in the first photograph, *front row, far right,* is touching at least three other people: the man and woman behind her and also the man in front of her. From these photographs, I think it's fair to conclude that she is affectionate, even sensual.

This photograph confirmed some of the observations I made from looking at the photograph on page 24. The same woman is the "heroine" of both photos.   COURTESY SAMUEL MENASHE

The quality about these photographs that made a deep impression on me is the air of melancholy that pervades both pictures. The two women in the first shot look infinitely sad, and the young man seems to be holding up his chin out of sheer bravado, as though he too would like to burst into tears. When I questioned the owner of the photographs, the son of the "heroine," he confirmed that this was a farewell photograph, taken at a time of permanent parting. The year was 1923, and the woman in the center of the photograph was about to leave her home town in Bessarabia to make the enormous journey to America, the New World. She had met a young man who was passing through her town on his way to America. They fell in love, and she decided to accompany him when he left, setting out together to seek their fortune in faraway lands. Years later, the woman's son, a poet, wrote this poem about his mother:

> *When my mother*
> *Was a young girl*
> *Before the War*
> *Reading sad books*
> *By the river*
> *Sometimes, she*
> *Looked up, wisely*
> *But did not dream*
> *The day I would*
> *Be born to her*

> —SAMUEL MENASHE

We've just looked at four photographs that contain important and meaningful pieces of information about the subjects and their lives. We've been able to make inferences based on close examination of the photographs, and when we checked those first impressions, they turned out to be correct. It's very important, incidentally, to verify the information you derive from reading and analyzing photographs. Never think of your first opinions as positive proof, because it's too easy, too often, to be mistaken. For as often as photographs can lead you to the truth, they can also lead you away from it. In fact, photographs always lie—at least in the sense that they never tell the whole truth. The clues they provide may lead you toward the truth or confirm a truth you already know. But they could also be misleading. So proceed cautiously with this sort of photographic analysis; it should be used only together with other sorts of investigative methods. A photograph records only a single instant—one brief, fleeting moment in time. That tiny instant, if it is typical, can often reveal a world of truly accurate information. But because it is so short, it doesn't do to rely on it alone. So, as you trace your family's history by way of its images, do get other sorts of evidence to corroborate your own observations.

Two photographs will show you what I mean. These photographs should prove to you, if you had any doubt, that photographs lie. What appears to be the truth is exactly that —an appearance of the truth!

The first photograph is of a family group, taken on the Greek island of Crete, around 1913. The young man at the upper right is the youngest son, and he is about to set off for the New World to seek the family fortune. (A familiar story. At no time was the melting-pot character of America more obvious to me than when I was going through the family albums of friends, colleagues, and strangers, looking for photographs for this book. Almost every collection included emigration from another country at some time or in some branch of the family.)

The second photograph (on page 30), taken a few years later, is of the same man. He is not quite so young, and he's no longer on a Greek island. Now he is on an American beach—in Long Island, New York, with his infant son. How American this proud young father looks! But when he was posing with his European family in their peasant dress with their peasant ways, he looked typically Greek—even though he, wearing city clothes, was dressed differently from the rest of the family. Here, on a beach in an American setting, he looks like a typical young American father of the 1920s, proudly displaying his infant son for the camera. We assume that the photographer is the baby's mother, since this is clearly a snapshot, rather than the work of a professional photographer. The photographer could, of course, be a family friend. But if so, where is the mother? Wouldn't she be somewhere close by such a young child? If she were not taking the picture, wouldn't she be in it?

COURTESY WILLIAM MAVROGIANNIS

The proud young father is the timid young man standing at the right on page 29. COURTESY WILLIAM MAVROGIANNIS

Now let's take a closer look. The clues to the real story are contained in the second photograph, the photograph of the young Greek immigrant as the new American father. As I looked closely at this second shot, I discovered (and you'll need your magnifying glass for this) that the father is the only figure on the beach not dressed in a bathing costume. He is wearing a white shirt, tie, and business slacks. Most of the people in the background are in bathing suits— old-fashioned, to be sure (the photo is fifty years old), but bathing suits nevertheless. This fact by itself is of little significance, but it does give us a clue that perhaps the father is not as at home, not as integrated into the American scene, as we at first thought.

The other thing I saw when I looked more closely is the

gingerly, stiff way he is holding the baby. He is not at all relaxed, not at all at home with the child. On the contrary, he is awkward in the way he handles it, holding it away from his body, as though it had been propped in place by somebody else—perhaps the same mysterious person who instructed the father not to move and then walked away. (Perhaps it was the mother.) The father is grimacing, he is not smiling, and he is not looking at the child at all. Instead, he is looking toward the photographer.

As to the baby: Despite the fact that it is being held by the father, it is completely isolated. The baby looks stiff and uncomfortable. It has nothing to hold on to, certainly not its father, and the look on its face is one of utter preoccupation with something very far away. The child looks as though it hardly knows where it is. This detachment is not uncommon for a much younger baby, but for this baby, who appears to be about a year old, it is totally atypical. Year-old babies grab, clutch, and yell.

In fact, this baby and father do not know each other very well. The baby has just been adopted, and the father is just beginning to learn his new role. The photograph was taken shortly after the baby was brought to his new home. This piece of information explains the strangeness that we see in the photograph. Father and son are awkward with each other because they are, in fact, strangers! The baby has not yet oriented himself, and the father is still clumsy and unsure with him.

All the elements we see in a photograph are small renderings of reality. But the composition that results when all the elements of a photograph are put together is not necessarily itself a reality. Or, to put it another way: Many small truths don't necessarily make one large truth. In the same way that a skillful novelist takes his or her raw material from reality —characters, scenes, and events witnessed or experienced —so also a skillful photographer arranges the elements of a photograph so that they appear as arrangements of reality, draped in an attractive way for the benefit of the lens and the people who will see the finished photograph.

Having issued the warning to beware of the ways in which photographs lie, let me now go on to talk about some of the things to search for when you are looking for truths about your family members.

Let's go back for a minute to the two photographs of Susan at summer camp. From studying Susan's posture, the way she was sitting, we derived an important piece of information about her, information that she herself corroborated. But how does one confirm this sort of observation if there is no Susan around to help?

One way is to look at as many photographs as you can find of the same person. These photographs may be shots that were taken within a short span of time, or over a period of years. A series of photographs can tell you a lot about habits, both physical and emotional.

Start anywhere. Study your subject's small physical mannerisms. How does the person hold his or her body? His or her head? Is it the same way consistently in a series of photographs? If so, there is probably a meaning to it, and perhaps you can find out what the meaning is. Look for other physical mannerisms—but beware of smiles. Don't assume because a person is always or often smiling that such a person is happy. A smile can mean many different emotional states, and often smiles—especially incessant smiles—can be a cover-up for tension, anxiety, anger, or other forms of unhappiness. Chances are that you will find someone who is constantly smiling, because *cheese* is the most photographed word in America. If and when this happens, scrutinize the rest of that person to see what else he or she is constantly and consistently doing. Study his or her hands in a series of photographs. Are they relaxed, loose, easy? Are they folded quietly in a lap? Are they twisted or knotted together; wound tightly around each other? Are the fists clenched, or the palms open? Are the hands upturned, or palms down? (Upturned palms are usually characteristic of generous, open people.) Are the fingers spread apart? Are the hands holding something—a book, a purse, a toy? If they are holding the same thing in a series of photographs, do you think this object may be providing some kind of security? Are the hands touching another person? How are they touching? Does the person have his or her arms around someone? Are they caressing or only resting? In other words, is the person a toucher (remember the photographs on pages 24 and 25)? If so, does he or she touch people, or objects? Somebody who consistently touches objects as opposed to people may be lonely and really looking for a person to touch.

What about posture? Does the person sit upright, slouch, lean against something, slump over? Are these one-time stances, or are they consistently appearing characteristics? Perhaps your subject is always sitting, even when others in the photographs stand. Or perhaps it is the opposite—he or she always stands, even when others are sitting. What might this indicate about your subject's health?

How does your subject hold his or her head? Straight up, held high, lowered, or tilted to one side? Are his arms open or folded across his chest? What about his legs? If your subject is sitting, are his legs open—spread or stretched out —or crossed? Open legs and open arms generally belong to a person who is open to the world—one who is friendly and who perceives the world as a friendly place, one who does not have secrets. Closed arms, or arms crossed against the chest, often belong to the person who is trying either to keep the world away from him or to keep the world from guessing his secrets. A person with crossed arms perceives the world, in some way, as an adversary. Many photographs of Richard Nixon taken during the last months of his presidency show him with arms resolutely crossed against his chest. Of course, crossed arms may mean that it's cold!

What are your subject's eyes doing? Do they always look

straight at the camera, or do they look down or off to one side? Do they look at someone else in the frame? Do they appear tense, worried, anxious, amused, affectionate, full of love, full of hate, angry, impatient, scornful, open, guarded, humorous, sour, serious, questioning? Your subject's eyes, more than any other feature, will reveal his or her true feelings. Cover the rest of the photo with your hand or a piece of paper and look at the eyes isolated from the rest of the face. Do the same in a series of photographs of a single person. Now what do you know about your subject? Is the expression fairly consistent? Or does it change from photograph to photograph? Are the eyes smiling in all the photographs? Does the smile reach the eyes?

Study your subject's clothes in a series of photographs. You will often find consistency in style and fashion. If your subject is a girl or a woman, does she most often wear a dress, skirt, slacks, or jeans? Is she usually dressed carefully or casually? Does she take an interest in how she looks, or is she careless and nonchalant? Could you describe her as a clotheshorse? How does she wear her hair? What does her dress tell you about her relationship to the opposite sex? About her athletic abilities or lack of them?

If your subject is male, apply a similar set of questions to him. Then look at the people around your subject. Is your subject usually alone, or usually in a group of people? What sort of group? Maybe most often there is just one other person. Is it usually the same person?

Ulla, the woman who is the subject of this series of photographs, avoids looking at the camera in all of them. In the first three, she is photographed with her mother, and with two elderly aunts. From looking at only the very first three in this series, we might conclude that she is a very considerate person and always looks to others to make sure that they're comfortable and happy. But in the last photograph, she has been shot against the background of an earlier picture of herself. If you look closely at this composite photograph, you will see that in neither of these does she confront the camera directly. Could our earlier conclusions be wrong? Could it be that Ulla is not as considerate as we first thought, but is only a very camera-shy person?

Are the photographs you are looking at mostly action shots? Candids? Or are they formal or informal portraits? Do you get the impression of an active and energetic person? Does he seem to have been dragged away from an indoor, sitting-still sort of activity to blink and stand stiffly in the sunlight and barely tolerate having his photograph taken? Does your subject seem to be in good health, or does she look as if she has been ill or is recovering from some sort of illness? Is your subject reluctant or eager, shy or aggressive? Is he or she usually front and center, or more often hanging back, hiding behind the other people in the photograph?

To those of you who say that it is the photographer who arranges the pose the subject will take, let me reply that this is true only up to a point. Very few photographers, and almost no amateurs, will attend to details such as clenched fists and head tilts. And as to the larger details, such as how a family groups or arranges itself, this is done, for the most part, by the subjects themselves, who fall into place almost subconsciously, rarely acting on any purposeful, thought-out decisions.

When they are preparing to have themselves photographed, a family group will automatically take positions next to one another in the way that makes them feel the most comfortable. Then the photographer will pose them within that grouping, by height, composition, harmony, etc. Since the photographer, if he is a professional, may not know the family members or their relationship to one another, such relationships will play little part in the way he groups the family for a collective portrait. More often than not, he will leave the basic group as it has arranged itself. And the odds are good that this arrangement is based primarily on psychological relationships. As such, it is worthy of some close observation.

Who is sitting or standing next to whom? Are they always photographed together? Do they always stand together when they appear in the same photograph? Do they look alike? Are they in love? Often, even if you didn't know beforehand that a couple was in love, you can tell instantly by looking at a photograph of them together. Sometimes what is not clear, or at least not obvious, in the flesh is extremely clear in a photograph.

If you see one young person imitating another, often the one doing the imitating is the younger.

Do the people in your photograph look at each other? Who looks at whom? Sometimes people can refer to each other without actually looking at each other.

In this photograph, which girl is doing the imitating?
ANNELISE WALLACH
ROSENBERG

This photograph, taken in 1899, is of four generations of women from a single family. They are great-grandmother, grandmother, mother, and daughter.

AUG. SCHMIDT, COLLECTION OF THE AUTHOR

The photograph of four generations of women from the same family is a subtle example of what I mean. I am convinced that the two women who are standing planned this photograph together, and I could swear that there's an ever so slight glint of amusement in their eyes as they think about the effect it will have on future generations of their family. They were right: These women are my foremothers, and I was very impressed when I found this photograph. I'll have more to say about it later on.

All the little quirks, habits, and expressions mean nothing if they appear only once or twice. But if they make themselves apparent again and again in photographs of the person you are interested in, you can begin, on the basis of these clues (and I'm sure you can think of others that I haven't thought of), to make some interpretations about the kind of personality you're looking at and about the role he or she plays in the family group.

Often individual family members assume or are assigned psychological or emotional roles with the unspoken permission of the rest of the family. These roles are never talked about by the family, and often they are not even consciously known about or recognized, either by the role player or his family. But nonetheless, they exist. For example, one sibling may be the clown of the family. Another might be the family clotheshorse (always preening in front of the mirror, always wearing exactly the right thing); yet another, the family beauty. Another, subtler and harder to pinpoint, might be the person who expresses anger and rage for the rest of the family. When a time comes that calls for anger, everyone in the family will look to that person to become furious on behalf of the entire family—everybody is feeling the anger, but only one has "permission" to express it. In this way the unpleasant task is taken care of for the rest of the family. Still another member might be the peacemaker or mediator, yet another the workhorse, and another the psychologist—the person who listens to everybody else's problems.

This is the sort of information you will never find in any written history of your family. However, if you look at enough photographs, it is sometimes possible to discern who plays what role—especially the more visual ones, like family clotheshorse or family beauty. If you see a particular pose, stance, expression, posture, attitude, or look repeating itself again and again in a particular individual, you may have stumbled upon one or another role being played in the family drama. Later on, when it is time to put your narrative together, you will want to confirm your observations by talking with someone who has either known your subject or known about him or her. This is the sort of information that probably no one would volunteer, but most people would be pleased—and surprised—to confirm it, if asked.

Human attitudes, emotions, relationships, and psychology are not the only sorts of information contained in family photographs. There is another kind of data there that is yours for the looking.

Study your family's clothes very carefully. In early, formal studio photographs, subjects dressed up specifically for the occasion. Even though the clothes might be "Sunday best," you can still gather a great deal of information about your subject's wealth, or lack of it—by carefully inspecting his clothes.

Do the clothes fit? Are they too big? Too small? Are they custom-made? If your subject is a child, were the clothes bought for her or him, or are they hand-me-downs from an older sibling or neighbor? Look closely at the wrists: Are they frayed? Are the sleeves turned? Do the sleeves end where they are supposed to? Are they too short? Too long? Are the shoes old and scuffed or new and shiny? The fit and condition of clothes and shoes will give you some good indications of the wearer's prosperity. It may be his only suit of good clothes, and even that may be ill fitting, old, or a hand-me-down.

It is not only what your subject is wearing, but also how she or he is wearing it that will afford you information. Does he wear his clothes with ease, or does he look out of place all dressed up?

Even if your subject's clothes do fit well, he may have only one such outfit. Look at a series of photographs of that person. See if he is always wearing the same outfit or always wearing different outfits. It helps to know something about his occupation: Was it farming, law, taxidermy? Then a series of photographs will give you some idea of how important posing for the camera was to him.

How many good outfits do you think the couple above owns?

How many good outfits do you think the couple at right owns?

This photograph is dated June 1911, before the invention of the electric washing machine. If these people did not have servants to do their laundry for them, you can be sure that they wouldn't have been so casual about sitting in the grass.

If the photograph is of a celebration of some sort, and everything is particularly fancy, and you know that the person giving the party—the one who paid the bills—was not particularly well-off, you can then judge how important— or unimportant—the occasion was.

Having looked at a number of photographs of this young man and his friends, I know that they were well-to-do and socially prominent. Therefore, I know that to show off clothes was not the reason this photograph was taken. The photograph was making another point: to show how popular the young man was with the ladies.

COURTESY MARY SCHIEFFELIN

Props and furniture can also disclose information about the life-styles in your family. Look again at the photograph of the four generations of my foremothers. After I had looked at the photograph many times, I finally noticed that the old lady is holding a book on her lap. A religious scholar, an acquaintance who happened to see the photograph, recognized the book at once. The book, he said, is a religious primer for Jewish women—a book of religious instruction given to Jewish women at that time (the photograph is dated 1899) because they were considered incapable of reading the Talmud, as the men did.

Because my great-great-grandmother chose to be photographed with this book in her hand, I assume that she was a religious person. This assumption was later confirmed for me by her granddaughter, who is my own grandmother. She said that she remembered the old woman only as a very religious old lady who "sat by the tiled oven all day and mumbled her prayers." This remark confirmed what I had thought, and it was also meaningful to me in another way. Because today my family is not at all religious, it meant a lot to me to learn that we once were. I would never have known this had it not been for a book in a photo and the confirmation provided by my grandmother's chance remark.

Until the invention in 1888 of the box camera, which was the forerunner of the Instamatic, most photographs were taken in studios. There were few "amateur" photographers as we know them today—in fact, the term did not exist. Photography was a cumbersome business, and the whole family was trundled off to a professional studio to be immortalized. The shooting area of the studio, the area where the picture was taken, often resembled a stage set. It was lavishly furnished with chairs, potted palms, drapes, fake staircases, and other objects of Victorian elegance. Later on, the furniture was replaced by painted backdrops.

The earliest of these studio photographs, which became popular after the Civil War, are called cabinet cards. The photographs measure roughly $3\frac{3}{4}$ by 5 inches and are mounted on $4\frac{1}{2}$ by $6\frac{1}{2}$ inch cardboard cards. If you find one of these in your collection of family photographs, you can be pretty sure it was taken sometime between 1866 and 1906. Each decade had its characteristic props and backgrounds. In the 1860s, the most common props were the balustrade, column, and curtain; in the 1870s, the rustic bridge and stile; in the 1880s, the hammock, swing, and railway carriage; in the 1890s, palm trees, birds, and bicycles; and in the early twentieth century, the motorcar, for snobs.

With a little hard looking, you ought to be able to tell whether the photograph in front of you was taken in a studio or in the home of a well-to-do ancestor. If you already know that the ancestor was a dairy farmer or a bricklayer, you can be pretty sure that the fancy chairs and the silk brocade tablecloth are studio props! (A hundred years

Left: *This is a cabinet card, a type of photograph popular in the last half of the last century. Notice how obviously fake the snow is. It is a painted backdrop.* WILLY FROHSINN, COLLECTION OF THE AUTHOR

Below: *This photograph was taken in the early twentieth century, when motorcars were fashionable studio accessories.*

COURTESY
RICHARD BLUMENTHAL

Willy Frohsinn

Düsseldorf
Königsallee 38-40

ago, the notion of taking photographs in the kitchen of a farmhouse was unthinkable, even if the photographer and his camera could travel. There aren't many examples of early "candid" photography, and many of the examples that do exist are in museums or academic institutions.)

Here is an early example of candid photography. In this photograph, dated 1909, the photographer was more interested in light, composition, and mood than in a flattering portrait of his subject. This photographer was years ahead of his time.

HUGO WALLACH, COLLECTION OF THE AUTHOR

Another way to get clues as to where the photograph was taken and information about the subjects' financial circumstances is to compare clothes with surroundings. Do they all go together? Do you think the clothes and the furnishings fall in the same price range? From the answer to this question and from the other information you already have, you should be able to make a reasonable guess as to whether the photograph was taken in a studio or not.

Chapter Four

How To Create
Your Own Album

❦

The best way to start collecting for a family album is with what you already have; start at home. Go through your attic, basement, and other storage places. Family albums, shoe boxes, old papers, boxes of odds and ends, scrapbooks, and Bibles are promising places to look for old photographs. They tend to get stashed away and forgotten in the most unlikely places, primarily because people don't know how to organize them, how to store them, or in general what to do with them. So they get sent to out-of-the-way corners (where they get brown and curly and faded), and that's where you should look first. When you're fairly satisfied that you've found what's available in your house, start organizing your find.

The first thing to do is to caption everything you can identify. By caption, I mean write a short paragraph, either *in pencil* on the back of the photograph or on a separate sheet of paper, naming the person or persons, the place, and the approximate date of the photograph. Add any other information you may have: the occasion or anecdotes about the persons in the photograph. Even if the anecdote doesn't exactly fit the photograph, if it is about the same persons, and if it happened at more or less the same time that the photograph was taken, add it on. With pictures of your immediate family, you'll need little or no help with this part of your captions, particularly if you yourself are in the photograph. For photographs that were taken when you were very small or before you were born, or with photographs you've gotten from distant branches of the family, you'll need help from other family members. Ask them very specific questions, either in person or by mail. When interviewing someone by mail, enclose a copy of the photograph you're asking about. Ask what day, month, and year the photograph was taken; where (address, city, and state); the occasion (someone's birthday, a family reunion, a wedding, athletic event, an anniversary, Christmas or other holiday, a christening or baptism, a meeting of the Odd Fellows, a gathering of all the people in a particular department at work). After you have all the hard facts and statistics, then ask for the kind of information that makes the project interesting from a human-interest point of view.

A different kind of family photograph. I learned from its owner (the son of one of the workers) that it was taken around 1937, in the Cumberland, Maryland, roundhouse at the railroad repair yards of the Baltimore and Ohio Railroad. COURTESY CALVIN KIIFNER

Find out, if you can, the name of the photographer and also anything special about the occasion: an interesting incident that happened earlier that day; who was wearing a new dress; who met who and later married; what happened a few hours after the photograph was taken—or another consequence of that particular day or event.

For the time being, store your material in file folders or envelopes to be assembled as an album when you've finished all your research. Probably the best way to file your material is under the subject's name. Keep a separate folder for each person whom you think will become a main character, and keep the folders together by family. Because you'll be dealing with so many photographs, you'll often have some decisions to make as to where a particular photograph belongs. Ask yourself, which of my characters is this photo really about?

As you assemble your preliminary collection, study the faces in front of you. Begin, slowly, to develop a personality profile of each subject. Who is this person? Again and again, as you confront someone who died a long time before you were born (and there probably will be many such faces), you'll find yourself beginning to regard him or her as an old friend. Make notes of your impressions and observations as you go along and file them with the photographs. Later on, you'll have a chance to compare your impressions with the opinions of others who knew, or still know, your subject personally. Your final description can be written in your album as a caption, either directly beneath the main photograph of the person or next to it. It might be a good idea to look for one main photograph of each person you plan to feature in your album, to use it as the opening photograph, like a chapter title. Sometimes the main photograph will be of an entire branch; sometimes it will include a number of individual people from different branches.

Write or visit other members and other branches of your family. Ask to look through their albums or shoe boxes. Most people, especially if they're relatives, will be pleased to show you what they have and to go through it with you. These snapshots are so personal (and they're often so bad, from both a technical and artistic point of view) that hardly anyone outside the immediate family ever wants to look at them. So, in a way, you're doing their owner a favor by asking! And you'll be doing him or her an even greater favor when you ask questions and make comments about the subjects and circumstances of the photographs. You might take a tape recorder along with you to avoid having to take notes during what may turn out to be a very personal conversation. Don't depend on memory (your own or anyone else's); it is notoriously unreliable.

The pictures you want to borrow are the ones that yield the most information about the people you're interested in —about their lives and about the quality and circumstances of life in general at the time the photograph was taken. From the borrowed photographs, have copy negatives and copy prints made (any lab, studio, or drugstore that develops film and makes prints will do this for you) and then return the originals to their owner.

During your research, you will come across some photographs that are in bad condition. They may be yellow, brown, torn, or faded with small black specks on them. Improper washing, faulty use of chemicals when the prints were originally made, or just plain age have gotten to them. The black specks are caused by the fact that the image itself has faded with the passage of time, but the original retoucher's marks are still as black as ever. The proper restoration of such photographs is best left to a professional restorer, which can be an expensive proposition. However, an old family photograph showing the passage of time is not an ugly thing as is a modern photograph that is damaged, and my suggestion is to leave it as it is. If the photograph is actually torn, have a copy print made to spare the original any more wear and tear.

As you pore over the contents of a shoe box or an album, helping their owner to sort through the contents, something extraordinary may happen. It will happen with many of the people you interview. You will come across one particular photograph, perhaps a series of photographs, that will unlock a memory. Without warning, you will find yourself the recipient of a flood of stories, an entire saga and drama of long ago. This is the very moment you've been waiting for. At last you will get rich information—answers to all the questions you asked and many that you didn't know how to ask. Looking at a class photo, an aunt, an uncle, or a great-aunt will suddenly begin to tell you about all the other people in the class. You will hear about long forgotten best friends, old favorite school clothes, books that were required reading in 1936, who had a crush on whom in the senior class. You will learn about the shortcut to school (there's an expressway there now), how long it took when there was snow on the ground, who was the best actor / poet / athlete in the class, and the name of the prettiest girl (she died nursing soldiers at the front in the Korean War).

It may not happen with everybody you talk to or with everybody whose photographs you look through, but sooner or later it will happen, and you should be prepared for it. Looking through old photographs invariably triggers memories, even if they don't come out in the flood I've just described. When they start—you can tell the symptoms from the look in the storyteller's eye—just turn on your tape recorder, sit back and relax; let the storyteller talk while you look, listen, and learn. Once started, most people don't need to have their memories jogged. Although what they tell you may not always be exactly what you want to know, you may, in fact, learn some fascinating things that you wouldn't have thought to ask about. In any case, you can edit your tape later on. Or you might want to include the story in your narrative more or less as it was told to you, with all the seemingly miscellaneous details which, to your surprise, you discover add lovely "local color" to your album. Now that you are hearing them, you realize that it is precisely the "unimportant" details that breathe life into any story, whether it be a family history or a mystery novel.

If there is something specific you want to know, you may have to return to a particular photograph more than once and ask for the information you want in a number of different ways before you get an answer. This is particularly true with older relatives, whose memories can be dull and tarnished one day and clear and bright the next, depending on the weather and the way you're asking the question. An incident that happened with my own grandmother is a good example of how fickle elderly memories can be.

My grandmother, born in Germany in 1883, had in her collection a fascinating class photo taken when she was sixteen at the finishing school in Lausanne, Switzerland, where her parents sent her for a year (a common practice among well-to-do German families at that time).

The year was 1899, and I was curious to know what the turn of the century was like—what it was like to be alive at that time and how she remembered the period. I asked her a number of historical and political questions which she didn't answer. She kept naming the other girls in the photograph; that seemed to be all she could remember about her year abroad. Finally, one day I asked her, "How did you celebrate New Year's Eve? Did you have a party?" Suddenly, there was an answer so good that I couldn't have dreamed up a better one. At last I had said the right thing, pushed the right button.

She said, "I remember wearing red, white, and black"—

To achieve that half-photographed, half-painted effect, this picture was made by taking the photo, then painting on the negative, then photographing the painted negative.

the colors of the German flag—"and writing a letter home to my father, saying, *Wir sind stolz auf unser Vaterland*: We are proud of our Fatherland."

Now this wasn't exactly the information I had been asking for, but in many ways it was much, much better. It told me all about how the German Jews (my grandmother was Jewish) felt about Germany before Hitler came to power. How ironic! They were proud to be Germans! It told me a lot about my grandmother's relationship with her parents. She was obviously close to them and closer to her father than her mother, as it was to him that she remembered writing. It also told me about how sixteen-year-olds once celebrated New Year's Eve.

If you are making your requests by mail, be specific about what you want. Otherwise, your relatives will probably send you photos that are pretty or flattering, but not very informative in the ways that matter to you. You might want to ask for:

1. Photographs of your subject at different ages. A sequence of photographs of one person at different times in his or her life will be very helpful and very interesting to look at, if you have room for a series.

2. Candid photographs—ones that catch your subject off guard. These will tell you more about personality, character, and life-style than will the formal, self-conscious ones. Besides, they're fun to look at.

3. Action photographs. Before the turn of the century, all photographs were posed and static, because a camera that could freeze action had not yet been invented. In these older photographs, the subjects had to sit still for so long (when you're sitting absolutely still, even five or ten seconds feels like an eternity!) that they acquired a frozen look. Sometimes that still quality gives the older photographs a look of deep spirituality, a look that newer photographs have tried to imitate, but without much success.

4. Photographs that show a variety of clothing. The more visible the details, the better.

5. Photographs of special occasions and rituals.

6. Photographs of houses, buildings, dwellings, rooms, factories, places of employment, summer camps and cottages, boats.

7. Pilgrimages to the New World, pilgrimages back to the Old Country, journeys to new and exotic locales.

8. Photographs taken in the kitchen and other out-of-the-way places.

You might want to prepare yourself by doing some background reading on the history of where you live, or the history of the immigration your family was part of, or the history of the times and events that you know affected their lives. Later, when you put your material together into a visual story (perhaps it will look a little like a comic book with dialogue and "stage directions"), you will want to include some of this supplementary material about the social, military, political, and religious atmosphere in which your forbearers lived, worked, wept, and loved. Put into your album any passages that you particularly like or that seem appropriate, or add some poetry to give your photographs a deeper and richer meaning.

Find out how your family made history. For history is made by ordinary people—chief cooks and bottle washers —much more than by generals, popes, kings, and presidents.

It will be easier to organize, and later on, to read, if you decide on one or more main characters for your album. Give your album a story line with a hero or heroine, as if it were a novel. Most often the main character in a family history is a grandmother or grandfather. Grandparents are the link between the past and the present; their lifetimes occasionally span as many as six other lifetimes, all the way from their own grandparents down to you and sometimes to the generation after you! Their lifetimes sometimes date from the pre-automobile, pre-electricity, and pre-telephone era to the space shuttle, video disks, and punk rock.

Families, when you're trying to chronicle them, often get out of hand. They grow so large, and there are so many people—sisters, uncles, cousins—that to have one or two central characters and to relate everyone else to them makes it easier for the reader to unravel family relationships. A grandparent makes a particularly good choice, not only for the reasons I've already given you, but also because there are usually more pictures of a grandparent in a greater variety of circumstances than there are of any other family member. Use a grandparent as an armature, or skeleton, on which to "hang" the rest of your story.

In addition to your central character, include also heads of households (or even the actual houses themselves) as main characters. If you have another branch, related by remarriage, include them too.

Families tend to come from one place, with one or more dwellings in that place, or from two or three central locations—for instance, the Washington, D.C., branch, and the Lexington, Kentucky, branch. One way to keep the different family branches straight is to identify them by their geographical locations.

Often these branches have occupied the same house for many generations. Houses used to stay in one family, handed down from parent to child through the generations, until circumstances forced a change. Today, however, fewer and fewer people can afford the upkeep of dwellings that were built to house large families with many children. Family homesteads are a dying tradition; they are disappearing as fast as large and stable families themselves are disappearing.

If you're lucky enough to have grown up in one place, your house may become one of your main characters, and the people who lived there once and who live there today,

A family homestead, the Pistone house in Rockland, Maine
COURTESY THOMAS THOMPSON

the featured characters in your story. A fictional example of such a homestead is TV's Little House on the Prairie. If your family homestead is still standing even though your family no longer lives there, you might want to go to visit it, photograph it, and include it in your album.

During the course of this project, you may come across a face that so captures your attention, so charms and delights you, that even though that person is of minor importance in the overall history of your family (say a distant cousin by marriage), you'll feel as though you *must* include him or her. By all means, do so; it doesn't matter how distant the kinship is. Sometimes the choices you make as the compiler of a family album will be different from the choices you would make as the compiler of a conventional family history or genealogy. Working with visual evidence is not the same as working with verbal evidence. Your raw material is different, and it is up to you to respect that difference, not ignore it. As a matter of fact you should emphasize it, honor it, and capitalize on it.

After you have gathered together all your pictures and the information that is to accompany them, it is time to start putting your album together. There are a number of ways to organize it into a colorful and effective book. There is no one best way, and there are no rules for doing it right. Your only guideline should be: Does it work?

Here are two suggestions.

1. Arrange your material according to family branches. For instance, if your father's family name is Walker and your mother's family name is Beebe, divide your album into three sections. The first two are called Walker and Beebe, with all the photographs from each branch in the appropriate section. In each include not only your appropriate parent and grandparents, but also distant branches from that side of the family. Reserve the third section of the album for the Walker–Beebe combination—you and your immediate family. Instead of a table of contents at the front of the book, draw a family tree to be used as a kind of road map, a guide to what can be found inside. Use a simple symbol, such as a particular leaf or fruit, to represent each branch. Throughout the album, the symbol will let the reader know which branch of the family he or she is looking at.

The old saying, "You can't tell the players without a scorecard" was never quite so true as it is when it comes to identifying and keeping straight the various branches of a family, even if the family is your own.

2. Another, simpler form of organization that isn't quite so all-encompassing or ambitious would be to put your story together in the form of *A Day in the Life of———*. In this format, you can still include practically every aspect of your family's life and its history by using flashbacks and flashforwards.

The caption for a photograph of someone cooking dinner might read as follows: *As Mama cooked dinner that night, she thought about her grandmother and the very different sorts of meals she had cooked for her enormous family.* This caption would then lead you right into a photograph of Mama's grandmother and her enormous family. Or under a snapshot of

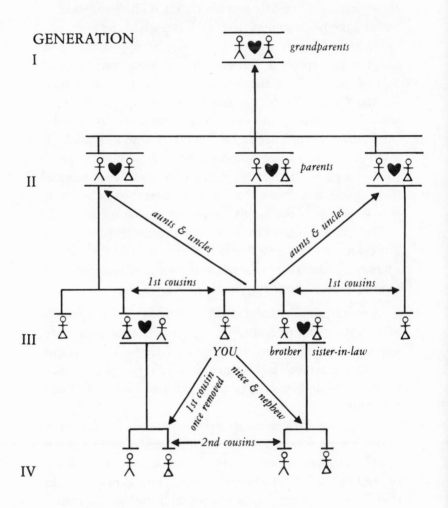

GENERATION

I

II

III

IV

grandparents

parents

aunts & uncles

aunts & uncles

1st cousins

1st cousins

YOU

brother sister-in-law

1st cousin once removed

niece & nephew

2nd cousins

Here is one way to diagram your family tree.

a family fishing trip, a caption might read: *Some of the other things we like to do on Sunday afternoons are . . .* From this caption, you can lead your reader into a wide variety of photographs of leisure-time activities.

Incidentally, as you compose and create your album, it isn't necessary to stick with the absolute truth at all times. If you feel like mixing a bit of fiction, a bit of storytelling with your facts, it will spice your story up and make it more fun both to read and to write. This is a particularly useful device if you discover that you can't get enough factual information about your photographs or the people in them. It is also a good idea if you happen to be more interested in writing a good story than in just telling the facts as they happened. A word of caution, though: If you do decide to mix in some fiction, be *sure* to indicate that you are doing so somewhere in the opening pages of your album.

As to the actual mechanics of putting pictures in your album: It depends on what type of album you are using. On cardboard or paper pages, use mounting corners or dry mount tissue. Mount photographs magnetically in albums made to hold them that way. What kind of album you use is up to you, but do not glue your photographs onto the pages themselves. Over time, glue will ruin your photographs.

It's inevitable that you'll find great gaps in your photographic narrative. There will be material missing: photographic material related to a particular period of time, a particular person, or one important branch of the family. There are several ways you can fill those gaps to make your story flow evenly. And you can combine different sorts of fill-ins.

Say, for example, that you're missing material from the years between 1890 and 1910. In the public library, read about what was happening in your particular area during those years. Pick one or two events with which your ancestors could have been involved. Write a brief description of those events, or find newspaper clippings from the time and place these in your album in place of photographs. You might even get a photocopy of a newspaper page of the time. In my own albums, I used such photocopies as background and put my personal photographs on top of them. The newspaper pages became literal backgrounds to the events and characters of my family. In terms of our everyday activities, this is in fact, what historical events actually do. They serve as background music—sometimes loud, sometimes very soft—and sometimes as both background and foreground to our lives, especially when what our family was doing on a particular day completely merges with a major historical event. For instance, probably most people in the United States can still clearly remember what they were doing on that awful day, November 22, 1963, when President John F. Kennedy was killed. Or one of the men in your family—say, a great-uncle—may have been in the navy and stationed in Hawaii in 1941. This fact would have been insignificant had not Pearl Harbor, Hawaii, been bombed by the Japanese on December 7 of that year, thus bringing the United States into World War II. However, your naval uncle became a meaningful part of history because of where he happened to be and what he happened to be doing on one of the most important dates in history. If you lived in New York City in 1977, chances are that you were a participant in the great New York City blackout. Thus, a newspaper clipping describing that blackout would be a perfect accompaniment to a group portrait or class picture taken in New York City during that year.

Various sources provide photographs for the asking—or at least for the price of making the print. You will have to use a little imagination (and perhaps some suggestions from your local librarian) to figure out where to write for what you want. Local chambers of commerce, state or government tourist offices, and local historical associations are some places to start.

Items other than photographs may be included in your album. You could create a collage of belongings, or use a single belonging: a report card, a dance card, a birthday card, a calling card, a wedding announcement, a handkerchief, a sash, a hair ribbon, a dried flower, a varsity letter, a lock of hair, a glove, or a fan. Or you could add newspaper clippings, passages from a diary, a letter written to or from someone in your family, personal poetry, or personal reminiscences.

Two ways of documenting your family. These collages are made by cutting up photographs and recombining parts. You could even use material from magazines or newspapers or include some belongings.

COURTESY LADUSKA ADRIANCE

Chapter Five

Taking Pictures
for Future Generations

One of the most satisfying aspects of putting together a family album is the fact that you, its author, automatically become an expert on the history of your family. You will also be taking your own photographs. In some ways, this means that you will determine how future generations will remember your family. Because what you are doing is so meaningful, so important, it pays to do it carefully and with forethought. Here are some suggestions, some things to be aware of, and some things to think about.

First and foremost, carry your camera with you even when you don't think you will be using it. Often the most memorable photographs in your collection will turn out to be the ones that were unplanned and unexpected.

As you carry your camera with you and as you shoot candid photographs, remember that you want to be as objective as possible. (True objectivity is never possible, but you want to come as close to it as you can.) With this in mind, do your best to be unobtrusive. This is not to say that you should try to hide either your camera or the fact that you're using it (such attempts usually end up attracting all sorts of attention), but unless you are posing a specific, formal photograph—say, a group portrait—the less you draw attention to yourself, the less influenced your subjects will be by your presence. The more inconspicuous you are, the closer you will move toward becoming a true historian. If your subjects don't realize that there's a camera in the room, then it won't occur to them to change their behavior to accommodate it.

Do your best to catch your family in unguarded moments.

BRIGITTE HANF ENOS

It is during unguarded moments that people act in ways that are most typical of themselves—in ways that are characteristic and unselfconscious. Not many persons are able to go about their business and just take no notice of someone following them with a camera. Chances are they'll mug, put up a big fuss, or tease. If this happens—and it probably will—the only way to deal with such interference is to simply outstay it. Just keep on shooting and shooting, right through it all. When at last they see that they can't either intimidate you or tease you out of it, they will probably get used to your presence and bored with teasing you, and go back to what they were doing. That will leave you a clear field to take as many photographs as you want. Now at last you can walk right into the middle of things, into the action. Now you can shoot from whatever angle and whatever position you please. Now you can get the photographs you want.

Keep your eyes open at all times. As you watch an event—a basketball game, a family picnic, a boat ride—unfolding, you can start shooting at any time. Take many, many shots and have small, wallet-size prints or contact sheets (also called proof sheets) made. From these, pick the best and most typical, have an enlargement made, and include it in your collection.

In keeping with the notion of making a truthful documentation, think about shooting in new and different ways. Instead of doing a group portrait of the entire Little League

An unusual travel shot; a "how I spent my summer vacation" picture. No question about where it was taken. Who do you suppose the photographer was? COURTESY MR. AND MRS. FRED WALLACE

team, why not stand behind the pitcher? Photograph his back, the batter's profile, and the catcher's face. Or photograph the locker room, before or after the game. Or shoot from second base while someone's stealing to third.

Instead of photographing the birthday cake when the birthday boy or girl is blowing out the candles, why not photograph it while it is still in the kitchen—while the batter is being mixed or as it is put into the oven? (If you were making a movie, this style of shooting would be described as a cinema verité approach.)

About posed, formal, and set-up shots: Say that you're setting up a formal photograph of your mother, father, three sisters, and two brothers. In your family, the boys have always been closer to their mother, and the girls to their father. They will probably arrange themselves according to this preference, but if, by chance, they should wait for you to tell them what you want, by all means suggest that the girls stand near the father (he might be sitting and they may be standing or vice versa) and the boys next to, or surrounding, their mother. If yours is a very outdoorsy, casual family, ask them to wear play clothes—jeans, sneakers, casual shirts or sweat shirts. Set up the shot in a place that is a natural habitat for your kin. Why not use a playing field, or a lawn, or even a nearby barn door as your backdrop?

This family has recently emigrated from Cuba to a heavily Cuban part of New York City. A concrete-and-graffiti playground is, for the moment, their only backyard. CATHERINE NOREN

Another possibility is to ask each member to hold a favorite item: tennis racket, doll, bicycle, briefcase, golf club, paintbrush, iron, broom, rolling pin, book, mirror—whatever is portable, visually interesting, and best represents the character and personality of its owner. Small children are often photographed with dolls and other toys. Why not have larger children—and adults, too—pose with meaningful objects or possessions? If you are a sit-around-the-dinner-table-and-chat sort of family, take your portrait around the dinner table. These environments will have meaning to the people who look at the photograph a week from now, as well as to future generations of your family.

If there is a specific element—object or person—that you particularly want to emphasize, put that element in the center of the frame, or front and center of the frame, and arrange the other elements around it. Or put that element to one side of the frame and arrange the other elements so that they direct the viewer's eye toward it. The closer an object is to the lens, the bigger it will appear in the photograph; the farther away from the lens, the smaller. If you have a camera with adjustable controls and are able to manipulate your depth of field, you can maximize or minimize the importance of an element in your frame by placing it very sharply in focus. Use an f stop of f / 2.8 or f / 4, and focus on the object or person you want to appear sharp. This will throw the other elements slightly out of focus, making them slightly blurred. People will assume more or less importance depending on whether they are near or far away, whether they are in sharp focus or slightly blurred, whether they are seated or standing, facing the camera, profile to the camera, or facing another person in the frame. If you want everything in the frame to be sharp, use an f stop of f / 16 or f / 11—and if you have enough light, a fast shutter speed as well ($\frac{1}{125}$ second or faster). As you make your decisions about these matters, you are actually translating all your information about your subject—psychological, emotional, and factual—into visual terms.

If you study photographs taken around the turn of the century, you'll notice that in many groups, the men are facing directly forward, while the women are turned 45 degrees, quarter profile to the camera. Today we would not hesitate to call this custom sexist and chauvinistic; it was done deliberately to emphasize the importance of the men and to minimize the importance of the women. The viewer was not permitted to see the women as clearly as the men because the women were thought to be of secondary importance, and their beauty, full face, might take our attention away from the men. You, however, could turn this practice to your own advantage; that is, place your most important character full face to the camera, with the others turned slightly toward him or her. Thus all eyes will be led toward the center of attention.

There are other ways to direct the viewer's attention where you want it. Place the lines of roads and fences, the edges of a boat's sail, etc. so that they lead into the photo-graph—to the left, right, up, down, out of the frame, or to the center of attention. Compose your image so that your viewer's eyes follow a visual path laid out by you. By doing this, you can determine what will be seen first and noticed most. How you compose your photograph will give you a great deal of control over how it will be seen and inter-preted.

A new and different kind of family photograph. Who are the members of this family? SUSAN SCHAEFFER

Just as everything counts in the photographs you look at, so everything counts in the ones you take. If somebody should walk into the frame as you are getting ready to shoot, wait until he or she leaves. If necessary, ask the person to leave. Twenty-five or thirty years from now, a person looking at your photograph might become very confused trying for hours or days to figure out who that stranger was, firmly believing him to be a member of the family. The same is true of dogs, cats, automobiles that happen to be parked in the wrong place or just driving through, and also stationary objects that you might be tempted to include either because they can't be moved or because you can't be bothered to move them. If the element is movable, move it. If it isn't, then move yourself and the camera. Or move your subject. Move whatever you have to move in order to get that unwanted element (such as a vase, a statue, bookshelves, or other items of household geography) out of your photograph. Otherwise it will be counted as symbolically meaningful. Because today we examine everything that appears in old family photographs, it is safe to assume that future generations will do the same with the photographs we take.

Because the cameras of a century ago required their subjects to be totally still and because photographs of that time were taken in a controlled environment, preparing to take a photograph was not unlike arranging a stage or theatrical set for a play. There was less chance that anything extraneous could accidentally creep into the frame than there is today. The ability to keep all extraneous elements out of the frame requires, first and foremost, a quality that may seem quite surprising—patience: the patience to wait until that dog, old woman, or small boy finishes making his way across your viewfinder and finally vanishes, leaving you and your photograph in peace. Then, too, you need the patience to wait until your subjects stop scratching, stop whispering to each other, stop rearranging their clothes, hair, makeup, etc. Then you need the patience to explain why you don't want your cousin's friend in the photograph (and for this you will also need tact). Most of all, you must have the patience to look; look carefully into all four corners of your viewfinder, and examine every single detail. Make sure that hands, folds of dresses, facial expressions, hair, groupings of people, animals, props, furniture and doorways, lamps in the background are arranged exactly as you want them. Make sure that the light is falling the way you want it to. If it isn't, turn on a light, turn one off, move a lamp closer to your subjects, or move your subjects closer to a source of beautiful and interesting light—a window, for instance. If you want a truly telling, meaningful, and significant family photograph, it won't do to overlook any detail, no matter how insignificant it seems. "I'll do it better next time" is not good enough. You may never have a next time.

The way the photographer has used light has changed this from a merely cute baby picture to a special photograph.

ANNELISE WALLACH ROSENBERG

Light is one of your most important considerations (the word *photography* means "writing with light"), and it is particularly important if you are shooting in color. In black and white photographs, all colors translate into tones of gray, but with color, the color of the light is very important. Make that fact your most important consideration as you decide which kind of film to use. If you want the color you see in the scene you're looking at to be part of your photograph, then use color film. If the colors you're looking at are not a vital element in the image you visualize, then

shoot it in black and white, because nobody really knows
how long color slides and color prints will last. (The first
color film was put on the market in the early thirties, and
the early color photographs have already faded badly. Despite the improved quality of the color film on the market
today, nobody really knows what its life will be.) Another
consideration is the fact that in photographs where the content is very, very important, as in family photographs, color
sometimes distracts.

If you're shooting outdoors, by natural light, the best
times of day for shooting are in the early morning and the
late afternoon. That's when the color of the light is most
interesting and the shadows most dramatic and photogenic.
In the middle of the day the sun is directly overhead and
casts ugly shadows, making black holes where eyes should
be and black shadows under noses. If you shoot outdoors
in the middle of the day, look for open shade where the
light is bright, but the shadows are soft.

Of course, the camera you use will make a difference to
the photographs you take. You can shoot with an Instamatic, a Polaroid, or a complicated camera with adjustable controls and interchangeable lenses. Each of these
choices has its advantages. If you shoot with a Polaroid, you
can see your photograph within seconds of shooting it. This
is wonderful for the impatient photographer and the impatient subject. If you don't like what you just shot, you can

reshoot it on the spot. Because you don't have to take many shots to make sure you got it right, Polaroid photography sometimes ends up being cheapest, although Polaroid packs are expensive to buy.

Using a 35mm (or larger format) camera with adjustable controls and interchangeable lenses has the advantage that you're actually able to manipulate your image while you're shooting it. For example, such a camera gives you the option of selective focusing. Selective focusing means that, by opening the aperture of your lens (setting the f stop to f / 2.8 or f / 4), you can make the parts of your photograph on which you focus your lens very sharp and for contrast, let the other elements or people in front and back of your subject appear soft to make them less obtrusive. On the other hand, if you want everything in your photograph to appear sharp, stop the aperture of your lens way down— that is, close it all the way to f / 16. This will have the same effect as squinting your eyes; everything in the photograph will be sharp.

Adjustable shutter speeds are another enormous advantage of cameras with adjustable controls. As adjustable f stops control the focus in depth—that is, from front to back in a photograph, adjustable shutter speeds control the sharpness, the focus on the vertical plane (right to left, left to right, top to bottom, bottom to top) in a photograph. A fast shutter speed—$\frac{1}{1000}$ or $\frac{1}{500}$ second—will freeze the

action of a speeding car or motorboat; $\frac{1}{60}$ or $\frac{1}{30}$ second—a much longer exposure—is all you need for sleeping or stationary objects—a baby taking a nap, a slumber party in the middle of the night, a Christmas tree before the action starts.

With a variety of lenses, you can magnify faraway objects, bring them very close, and eliminate unwanted elements from the frame. You can also look microscopically close at the texture of skin, a single eye, and other such isolated elements. With a wide-angle lens, you can make close objects very large indeed, while only slightly more distant ones appear very small. You can drastically change the size of the elements in your photograph by very small adjustments in the distance you place them from your camera.

On the other hand, an inexpensive camera without controls has the enormous advantage of speed. There is nothing to set, nothing to adjust, nothing to manipulate; you just aim and shoot. For this reason, it is not only the least noticeable, it is also the simplest to operate.

The subject matter and the photographer are what really count. These two elements will make all the difference as to whether you will get a photograph that speaks clearly to future generations of your family.

Opposite: *Because every detail in this formal portrait was important, the photographer probably used an aperture of f/16 or more to make sure that everything would be in very sharp focus.*

COURTESY VIRGINIA BUCKLEY

Chapter Six

A Long and Satisfying Life—
A Grandmother's Story

Meta Strauss Wallach was my maternal grandmother. Maybe because she lived longer than anyone else in the family, she was the most photographed member. She lived to be ninety-four, finally dying, in December 1977, of extreme old age. Her lifetime spanned two continents and both world wars; the inventions of cars, planes, television; and the landing of the first man on the moon.

Meta Strauss, born on April 12, 1883, was the fifth of seven children. Her father, Samuel Strauss, owned a millinery store in Bochum, an industrial town in northwest Germany.

Samuel was a very strict father, and as a result, his daughters had a spotless reputation in Bochum. Once, in a rare act of defiance, my grandmother cut a hole in her stocking. She was locked in her room for an entire day.

Samuel's strictness was probably the reason why his sons were so passive and indecisive. This trait was to lead, later, to the tragic deaths of all three of them.

Samuel, my great-grandfather, was also very wealthy. Because he was able to provide each of his daughters with a large dowry, they were able to marry well.

By the time she was twenty-five, Meta was quite anxious to get married. (Twenty-five was considered quite "elderly" in those days.) She was introduced to Moritz Wallach (my grandfather-to-be) by mutual cousins on a turn-of-the-century version of a blind date.

Moritz was looking for a wife, Meta was looking for a husband, and since they liked each other when they met, they saw no reason to wait. They announced their engagement on the day after they met! (Their marriage was to last for fifty-five years, until Moritz died in 1963.)

Now, for purposes of comparison, let's skip ahead in time for just a moment, to look at two other wedding photographs from later generations of the same family.

If you compare these three generations of wedding photographs, you can get a good panorama, in capsule form, of how our customs and manners have changed from generation to generation (see pages 96 and 97).

After their wedding in 1908, Moritz and Meta lived in Munich, where Moritz started an antique business, and

Meta raised their children; in addition to Annelise (who was actually the youngest), there were three others: Rolf, Lotte (my mother), and Fritz.

The time was the 1920s, and for the Wallachs and their children, it was the best, the most prosperous, and the most peaceful of times.

In 1928, Moritz and Meta's oldest son, Rolf, came to the United States. This is how it happened: When Rolf turned eighteen, Moritz invited him to sit in on business meetings. At the first meeting Rolf attended, he opened his mouth to say something, and Moritz told him to be quiet; he wasn't actually supposed to participate. Rolf did as he was told and sat quietly for the rest of the meeting. When it was over, he got up, walked out the door, and went directly to the American consulate, where he applied for a visa to come to this country.

Rolf had no intention of staying in America; his plan was eventually to go back to Germany to live. But after Hitler became chancellor of Germany in 1933, Rolf's plans were to change. By the middle thirties, he could see how dangerous it was for his family to stay in Germany, and he was instrumental in helping them all to get out.

As dictator of Germany, Hitler built up the country's military strength by rearming her, and he unified the people through fanatic speeches, gaudy propaganda, and unbridled nationalism.

The Nazis made life unbearable for Germany's Jews.

They stole their businesses, stole their private possessions, and threatened their lives. Rolf helped his family to get out of Germany, to get to the United States. Because Meta's brothers couldn't decide to leave Germany, could not bear to leave home, they died in Nazi concentration camps.

Moritz and Meta fled to New York, where they moved into a tiny apartment. Refugees fleeing from Germany were not allowed to take any money out of the country; the Nazis kept the Wallachs' business and their bank account as "escape tax." Moritz and Meta arrived in New York with the equivalent of ten dollars to their name. Moritz started work. Meta worked too. She had never worked before.

Moritz and Meta's children had also come to the United States. They married in this country and soon started having children of their own.

My grandfather Moritz died in 1963, but Meta lived on, and remained in good health and good spirits for another fourteen years.

On the following pages 90–109 is a scrapbook of photographs featuring my grandmother Meta, her children and grandchildren.

Meta, **left,** *with some of her brothers and sisters in a daguerreotype, the earliest kind of photograph.*

❦

Opposite: *My grandmother as a fifteen-year-old. This photograph was taken by a friend who sent it to my grandmother in the form of a postcard. The message is:* Greetings from Bochum from a secret admirer.

Above: *The back of the postcard yielded a lot of information. From the postmark, I got the date of the photograph (November 1, 1898), which told me my grandmother's age; I learned her street address; and I learned how much it cost to mail a postcard in 1898.*

Above: *The Strauss family, 1903. Meta, my grandmother, third from right, is standing, as are all the other women. Her father, Samuel, second from left, and all the other men are seated. In this photograph, the women are in profile, and the men full face, to show that they are more important.*

Opposite: *The Strauss family as they looked in 1920. Seventeen years after the first photograph was taken, Meta and her family got together (it was the youngest son's wedding day) and posed for another photo in the same way. To make sure you didn't miss the point, they placed the 1903 photograph front and center.*

Above: *Moritz and Meta on their wedding day, September 20, 1908. It doesn't take close examination to see that these two people aren't very comfortable with each other. And why should they be? They barely know each other, and here they are, committing themselves to a lifetime together.*

Opposite: top, *In 1943, in New York City, Moritz and Meta's youngest daughter Annelise married Howard Rosenberg. This is their wedding photograph.*   SHULAMITH STEIN

Bottom: *In 1970, Annelise and Howard's daughter Yvonne was married on Long Island to Mitch Relin. This is their wedding photograph.*   CATHERINE NOREN

Above: *Moritz and Meta were very proud of their four children, as large families, by that time, were rare. They were always bundling them off to the photographer's studio. My mother, Lotte, left, remembers the day this photograph was taken: She was equally proud of her new turquoise ring and her new sister, Annelise. She managed to display both!*

Opposite: top, *Because they lived in Munich, the Bavarian Alps lay right outside their doorstep. The family loved mountain climbing and skiing.*

Bottom: *My grandparents wanted their children to experience the pleasures of the beach at least once. And so, during the summer of 1924, they undertook the two-day journey from Munich, Bavaria, to Wangerooge, in the Frisian Islands in the North Sea. Everyone remembers it as a wonderful summer.*

Opposite: *The Wallach family in their garden in 1928, shortly before Rolf,* far right, *came to America. This photograph tells something about each member of the family: The men, Moritz and Rolf, are standing protectively on each side of the family. Meta, the mother, is the only one privileged to have a chair. Annelise, the little girl on the well, is still a child, so she's allowed to wear a bathing suit for the photographer. Lotte (my mother) has turned seventeen. She's just met the man who would later become my father, and look at the dazzling smile on her face! Fritz, the teenager (he's fourteen), in the lederhosen (Germany's onetime answer to Levi's), is the only one who looks as though he'd rather be somewhere else.*

Above: *Rolf in New York, around 1928*   ERICH SCHAAL

This is Moritz Wallach's antique store in Munich on a day when Hitler was having a parade. All the store windows in town had to be draped in order not to distract any eyes from the spectacle that was Hitler.

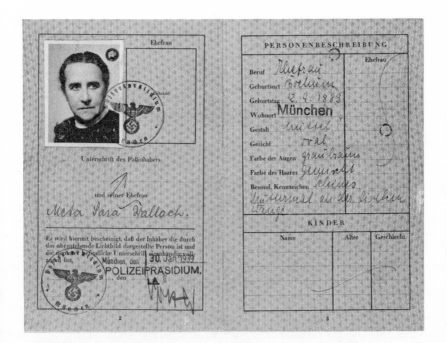

This is my grandmother's passport. Fear and anxiety are visible in
her face. Look at her signature: All Jewish women were forced by
the Nazis to take the middle name Sara; all Jewish men were forced
to use the name Israel.

My grandmother at her sewing machine. To her surprise, she enjoyed working. Compare her expression in this photograph to the one on her passport.

Fritz, standing left, *his wife Lucille,* seated center, *and their two boys; and Annelise,* seated right, *her husband Howard,* standing right, *and their daughter Yvonne. This photograph was taken around 1951. Compare this photograph to the photos on page 97 of Annelise and Howard's wedding and their daughter Yvonne's wedding.*

Above: *My grandmother always loved babies. Here she is with one of her six grandchildren. She even put on her glasses for the occasion —something she rarely did (she managed to keep both her vanity and her good eyesight for most of her life).*

ANNELISE WALLACH ROSENBERG

Opposite: *Here are Moritz and Meta on September 20, 1958. It was their fiftieth wedding anniversary, and they celebrated it surrounded by their children and grandchildren. It was a family reunion, a day of great happiness. Compare this photograph with the photo on page 96, taken exactly fifty years before.*

ANNELISE WALLACH ROSENBERG

On April 12, 1976, Meta Strauss Wallach became ninety-three years old. Here she salutes the photographer with a glass of prune juice. After all these years, my grandmother had lost none of her sparkle. CATHERINE NOREN

Bibliography

Akeret, Dr. Robert V. *Photoanalysis*. New York: Pocket Books, 1975.

The Family of Children. New York: Grosset & Dunlap, A Ridge Press Book, 1977.

The Family of Women. New York: Grosset & Dunlap, A Ridge Press Book, 1979.

Gallagher, Dorothy. *Hannah's Daughters: Six Generations of an American Family*. New York: Thomas Y. Crowell, 1976.

Hirsch, Julia. *Family Photographs: Content, Meaning, and Effect*. New York and Oxford: Oxford University Press, 1981.

Jury, Mark and Dan. *Gramp*. New York: Penguin Books, 1978.

Lartique, Jacques H. *Diary of a Century.* New York: Penguin Books, 1978.

Lesy, Michael. *Time Frames: The Meaning of Family Pictures.* New York: Pantheon Books, 1980.

———. *Wisconsin Death Trip.* New York: Pantheon Books, 1973.

Lichtman, Allan J., and Challinor, Joan R., eds. *Kin and Communities: Families in America.* Washington, D.C.: Smithsonian Institution Press, 1979.

Noren, Catherine Hanf. *The Camera of My Family.* New York: Alfred A. Knopf, 1976.

Steichen, Edward. *The Family of Man.* New York: Simon & Schuster, 1967.

Zeitlin, Steven; Kotkin, Amy; and Baker, Holly Cutting. *A Celebration of American Family Folklore: Tales and Traditions from the Smithsonian Collection.* New York: Pantheon Books, 1982.

Index

Page numbers in *italics*
refer to captions.

About the Author

Author CATHERINE NOREN says: "I was born in Germany but left when I was a few months old. I never knew much about my family or about my own history. One day, by accident, I found a drawer full of old photographs which were beautiful, mysterious, and filled me with curiosity about my own roots. With these photos of unfamiliar ancestors in front of me, I learned to study and analyze images and to find their meaningful clues. I started interviewing long lost family members and suddenly I had uncovered a whole history." The results of the author's search were published in a book called *The Camera of My Family.*

Both a writer and a documentary photographer, Ms. Noren is also the author of *Photography: How to Improve Your Technique,* as well as numerous magazine articles and photo essays. She has had one-woman shows in Milan, Italy, and New York City. She lives in New York.